I feel...

 happy

 calm

 sad

 angry

 worried

 confident

 scared

 surprised

 disgusted

 unsure

 excited

 embarrassed

 panicked

 focused

 disappointed

 silly

 friendly

 jealous

 bored

 muddled

 tired

 unwell

 hungry

 hot or cold

How do I say "I feel calm" in Makaton?

I feel

Take one hand with your thumb pointing upwards and your middle finger pointing to your chest. Bring your hand upwards and say, "I feel".

calm.

With a calm look on your face, hold your hands flat with palms facing down, make a circular movement and say, "calm".

ISBN 978-1-78270-692-2

Copyright © Channon Gray

All rights reserved. No part of this publication may be reproduced or utilised in any form or by any means electronic or mechanical, including photocopying, recording, or by any information storage and retrieval system now known or hereafter invented, without the prior written permission of the publisher and copyright holder.

No part of this book may be used or reproduced in any manner for the purpose of training artificial intelligence technologies or systems. In accordance with Article 4(3) of the DSM Directive 2019/790, Award Publications limited expressly reserves this work from the text and data mining exception.

First published 2026

Published by Award Publications limited
The Old Riding School, Welbeck, Worksop, S80 3LR

awardpublications @award.books
www.awardpublications.co.uk

25-1206 1

Printed in China

All About Calm Scribble

Written and illustrated by
Channon Gray

award

When we are calm, our BIG feelings take flight.

We feel safe inside and the world feels light.

Calm feels like a gentle breeze on a warm spring morning.

Your brain feels clear,

your heart beat is steady

and your muscles start relaxing.

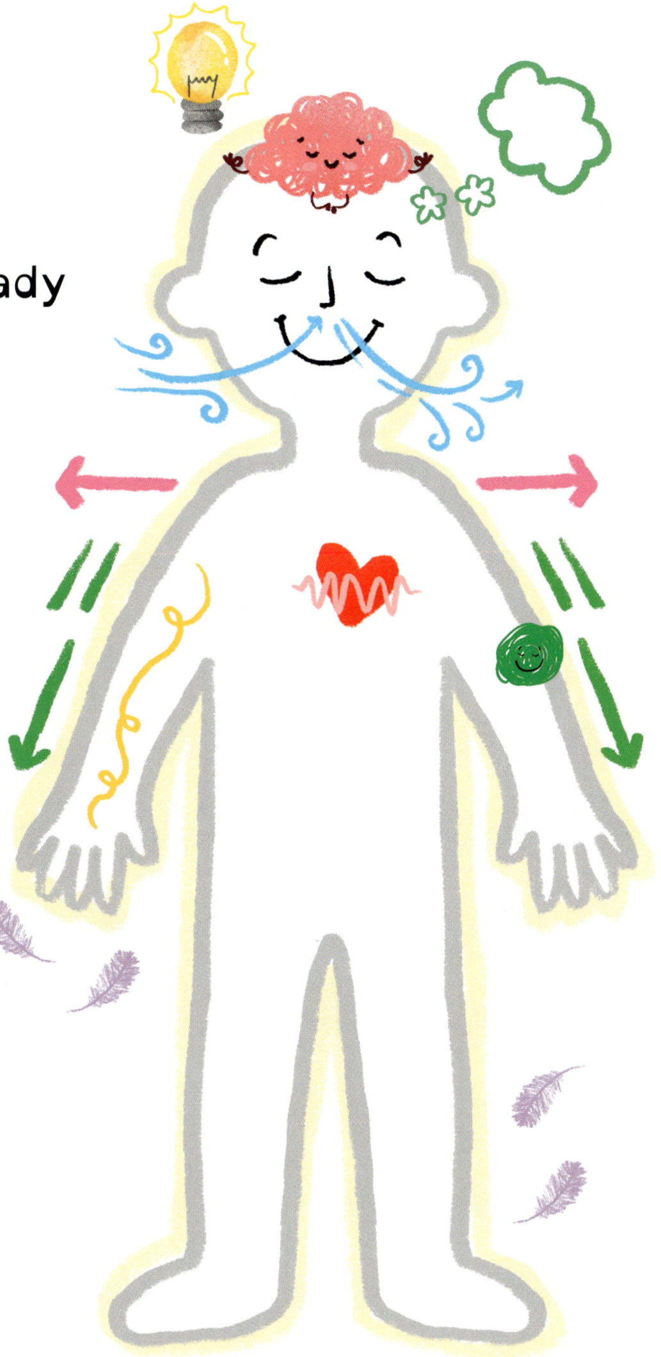

What can you spot?
I am Spot-It Scribble.

Being calm feels and looks different for everyone.

It can help you want to learn new things...

...and get along with your friends.

Or manage emotions as they bubble up,
so you can have more fun.

Feeling calm gives our

bodies

and brains

time to **rest** and **recharge.**

It makes it easier to think, solve problems and make decisions that normally might feel quite hard.

When we feel calm, we can manage
BIG feelings better and feel more in control...

I can choose my actions!
I am In-Control Scribble.

...even when things get tough
and look like they are about to unroll.

It can be soft,

or it can be strong.

With calm in your body and mind,
you feel you belong.

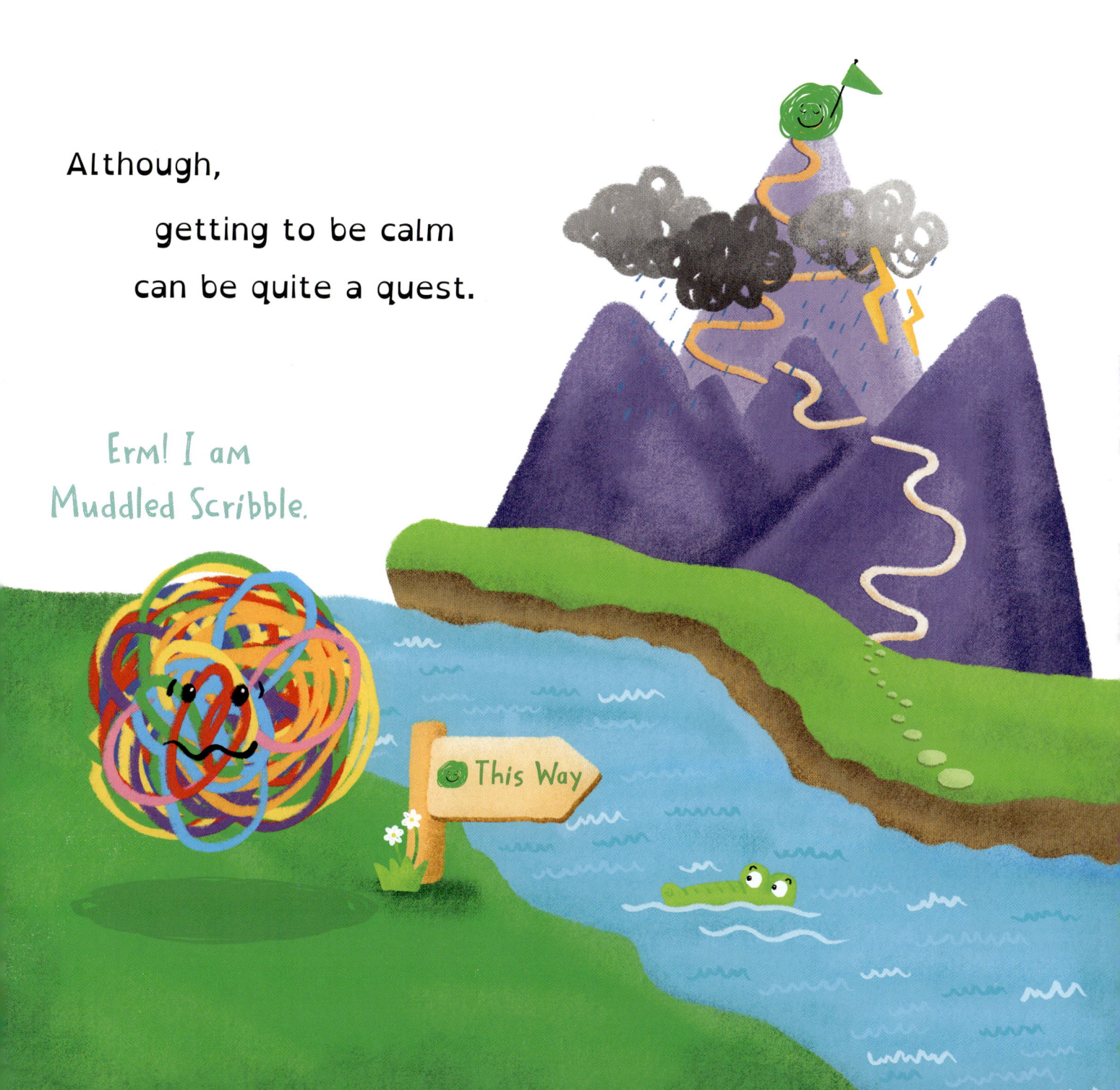

Although,
getting to be calm can be quite a quest.

Erm! I am Muddled Scribble.

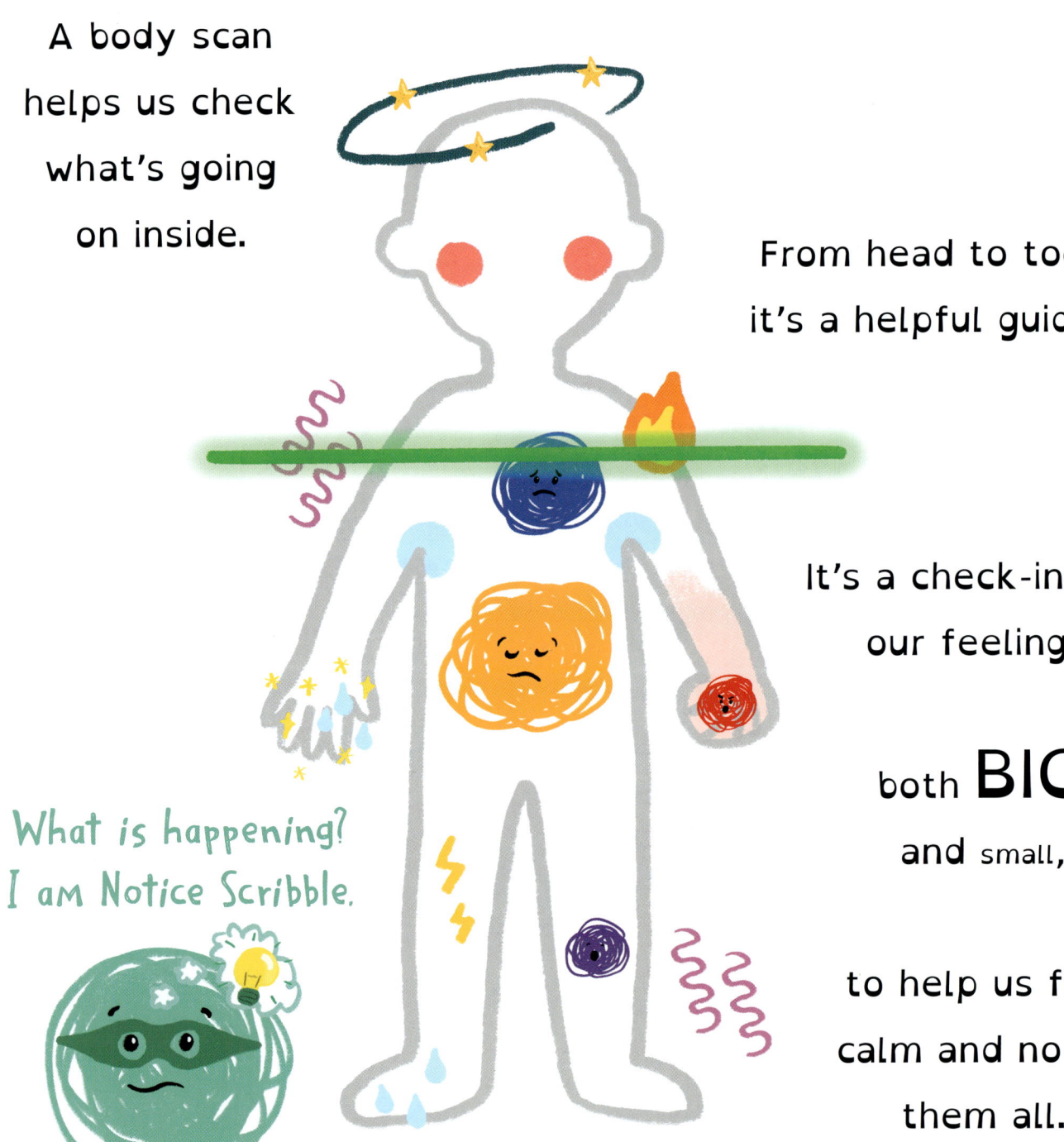

Close your eyes softly,
slowly breathe in and breathe out.

Notice what is happening in your body. Is it calm, or does tension need to break out?

Scan from the top of your head all the way down to your toes.

Feel each part relax as the calmness flows.

Imagining a happy place can calm your brain and your heart.

It gives you a moment to feel safe and make a fresh start.

It's like a pause button
for when life feels too fast.

Our happy place helps us feel calmness and peace that lasts.

Imagine holding a big
mug of hot chocolate,
all warm in your hands.

Breathe in the sweet
scent through your nose,
notice your lungs swell
as they expand.

Feel the warmth
fill your whole body,
before breathing out slow.

Blow on your cocoa,
letting your calmness grow.

Let's take a moment!
I am Breathe Scribble.

Mindful drawing is doodling with care.

Draw lines, shapes and patterns; notice calmness in the air.

Stretch like a cat,
then reach to the sky.

Stand like a
flamingo, and feel
calm nearby.

Breathe in and out,
with each step
you take.

Yoga helps you feel peaceful,
with each pose you make.

It helps you feel calm and steady inside.

Like a hug for yourself,
it's gentle and kind.

Sometimes keeping calm can be tricky, especially when BIG feelings loom large.

But, with practice...

...calmness can quickly recharge!

When we're calm,
the world just feels right.

We can take a deep breath,
which helps us feel relaxed and light.

Feeling safe, settled and calm
allows our smile to peek.

Calm Scribble Activities

Fill a bottle with water, glitter and clear glue. Put the top on tightly and shake it. As you watch it settle, feel calmer in your body and mind.

Create your own 'Calm Corner' with a cushion, blanket, toys or a calm picture. Or imagine a restful space in your head!

Go for a walk outside. Notice five things you can see, four you hear, three you touch, two you smell and take one deep breath.

The Scribbles Crew love to see your creations! Ask your grown-ups to share them on social media using #TheScribblesCrew

Scan the QR code on the back cover for more great Scribbles Crew activities, sing-along songs and teaching resources specially created by The Exciting Teacher.

www.thescribblescrew.com